WORDLY WISE 3000®

Systematic Academic Vocabulary Development

Cheryl Dressler

W9-CKC-017

Book **K**

School Specialty, Inc.
Cambridge and Toronto

Acquisitions/Development: Kate Moltz
Editor: Laura A. Woollett
Executive Editor: Bonnie Lass
Senior Designer: Karen Lomigora
Illustrators: Bryan Langdo, Hannah Bureau, and Jannie Ho

Printed in Beauceville, Québec, Canada, in July 2012
ISBN 978-0-8388-2818-2

8 9 10 TRN 15 14 13 12

Dear Boys and Girls,

Welcome to Wordly Wise 3000 Book K!

Your teacher will read you some stories and help you do some activities, too. You will learn lots of new words.

Have fun!

Story Words

muddy

soil

join

ring

slip

stare

row

dew

strong

fluffy

Directions: **Have children look at the pictures as you read the story aloud.**
Then have them mark items in the pictures related to muddy, soil, join, ring, and slip.

Directions: Have children paste the pictures in the order they happened.

Directions: Have children find and color pictures related to **stare**, **row**, **dew**, **strong**, and **fluffy**.

1. join

2. soil

3. muddy

4. dew

Directions: **Have children circle the picture that matches the word you say.**

Directions: Have children connect the **fluffy** animals.

Story Words

wave

tiny

wiggle

insects

creep

community

destroy

healthy

signs

peaceful

Directions: **Have children look at the pictures as you read the story aloud.**
Then have them mark items in the pictures related to wave, tiny, wiggle, insects, and creep.

2

3

Directions: Have children paste the pictures in the order they happened.

Directions: Have children find and color pictures related to **community**, **destroy**, **healthy**, **signs**, and **peaceful**.

11

1. tiny

2. creep

3. sign

4. wave

Directions: Have children circle the picture that matches the word you say.

Directions: **Have children use a green crayon to connect the things that have been destroyed and a purple crayon to connect the insects.**

What Do You Know?

1.

2.

3.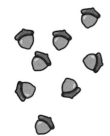

4.

5.

6.

Journal

Story Words

glance

empty

leak

split

float

collect

cradle

burst

flat

patch

Directions: Have children look at the pictures as you read the story aloud.
Then have them mark items in the pictures related to **glance**, **empty**, **leak**, **split**, and **float**.

2

3

Directions: Have children paste the pictures in the order they happened.

Directions: Have children find and color pictures related to **collect**, **cradle**, **burst**, **flat**, and **patch**.

19

1. float

2. leak

3. split

4. cradle

Directions: **Have children connect the carrots to get the bunny to the lettuce patch.**

21

What Do You Know?

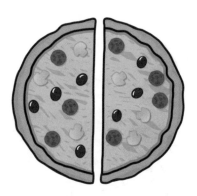

Journal

Directions: Have children draw a picture of something they **collect** or would like to **collect**.

23

1

Story Words

rotten

stumble

rope

edge

invitation

blame

able

glossy

polite

naughty

Directions: Have children look at the pictures as you read the story aloud.
Then have them mark items in the pictures related to **rotten, stumble, rope, edge,** and **invitation.**

2

3

Directions: Have children paste the pictures in the order they happened.

1. rope

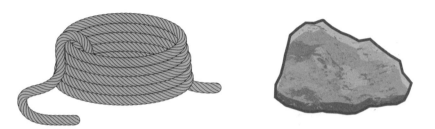

2. stumble

3. edge

4. glossy

Directions: Have children circle the picture that matches the word you say.

Directions: Have children connect the pictures of things they are **able** to do.

29

What Do You Know?

1.

2.

3.

4.

5.

6.

Directions: **Have children circle the picture that matches the word you say.**

Journal

Directions: Have children draw an **invitation** to a party.

1

Story Words

rub

crowd

fit

delighted

stretch

office

patient

proud

tools

sight

Directions: Have children look at the pictures as you read the story aloud.
Then have them mark items in the pictures related to **rub, crowd, fit, delighted,** and **stretch.**

Directions: Have children paste the pictures in the order they happened.

FLHP 10
ZNET 20
QDTZ 30
PBXR 40
MYAX 50
KRVN 60

DR. LEE

Directions: Have children find and color pictures related to **office**, **patient**, **proud**, **tools**, and **sight**.

35

1. tool

2. office

3. stretch

4. fit

Directions: **Have children circle the picture that matches the word you say.**

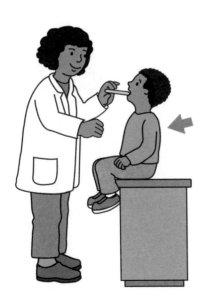

Directions: **Have children use a red crayon to connect the patients and a blue crayon to connect the children who look delighted.**

37

What Do You Know?

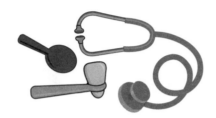

Directions: **Have children use the correct crayon to circle the picture that matches the word you say.**

Journal

Directions: Have children draw a picture of a **proud crowd**.

39

1

Story Words

surprise

whisper

present

decorate

lump

giggle

frown

plenty

straight

relax

Directions: Have children look at the pictures as you read the story aloud.
Then have them mark items in the pictures related to **surprise**, **whisper**, **present**, **decorate**, and **lump**.

Directions: Have children paste the pictures in the order they happened.

FARMER FOSTER'S SILLY FARM

Directions: Have children find and color pictures related to **giggle**, **frown**, **plenty**, **straight**, and **relax**.

43

1. straight

2. decorate

3. present

4. frown

Directions: **Have children circle the picture that matches the word you say.**

What Do You Know?

1.

2.

3.

4.

5.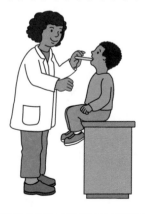

6.

Directions: Have children circle the picture that matches the word you say.

Journal

Directions: Have children draw two pictures: something that would make them **giggle** and something that would make them **frown**.

47

Story Words

dangle

chilly

straw

instruments

whistle

fresh

poke

sniff

practice

den

Directions: Have children paste the pictures in the order they happened.

Directions: Have children find and color pictures related to **fresh**, **poke**, **sniff**, **practice**, and **den**.

51

1. sniff

2. den

3. straw

4. instrument

Directions: Have children circle the picture that matches the word you say.

Directions: **Have children connect the things that are chilly.**

What Do You Know?

Directions: **Have children use the correct crayon to circle the picture that matches the word you say.**

Journal

Directions: Have children illustrate the two meanings of the word **straw** or **den**.

1

Story Words

melt

balance

bounce

sparkle

full

trade

top

drain

dusty

shady

Directions: Have children look at the pictures as you read the story aloud.
Then have them mark items in the pictures related to **melt, balance, bounce, sparkle,** and **full.**

2

3

1

2

3

Directions: Have children paste the pictures in the order they happened.

Directions: Have children find and color pictures related to **trade**, **top**, **drain**, **dusty**, and **shady**.

59

1. balance

2. shady

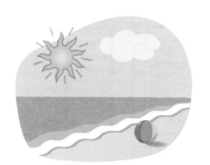 

3. top

4. full

Directions: **Have children circle the picture that matches the word you say.**

Directions: **Have children use a red crayon to connect the things that sparkle** and a blue crayon to connect the things that are **melting.**

61

What Do You Know?

1.

2.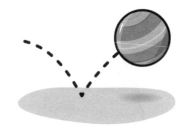

3.

4.

5.

6.

Directions: Have children circle the picture that matches the word you say.

Journal

Directions: Have children draw a basket that is empty. Then have them add things to the basket to make it **full**.

63

1

Story Words

cushion

touch

smooth

metal

silky

include

comfort

stroke

hard

gentle

Directions: Have children look at the pictures as you read the story aloud.
Then have them mark items in the pictures related to **cushion, touch, smooth, metal,** and **silky.**

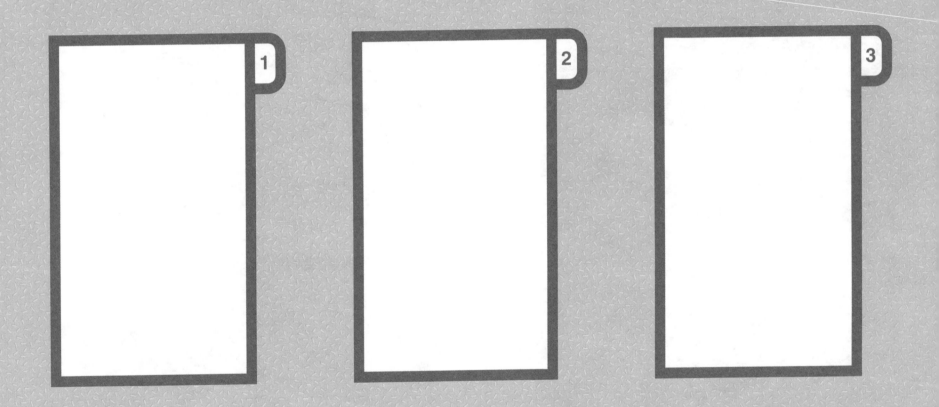

Directions: Have children paste the pictures in the order they happened.

Directions: Have children find and color pictures related to **include**, **comfort**, **stroke**, **hard**, and **gentle**.

1. cushion

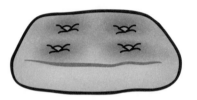 

2. comfort

3. stroke

4. hard

Directions: **Have children circle the picture that matches the word you say.**

Directions: **Have children use a red crayon to connect the things that are made of metal and a green crayon to connect the things that are silky.**

69

What Do You Know?

Directions: **Have children use the correct crayon to circle the picture that matches the word you say.**

Journal

Story Words

sting

beak

blossoms

pair

fear

brave

protect

store

miserable

wing

Directions: Have children look at the pictures as you read the story aloud.
Then have them mark items in the pictures related to **sting, beak, blossoms, pair,** and **fear.**

Directions: Have children paste the pictures in the order they happened.

Directions: Have children find and color pictures related to **brave**, **protect**, **store**, **miserable**, and **wing**.

75

1. beak

2. blossoms

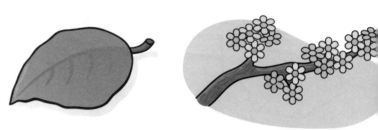

3. pair

4. miserable

Directions: **Have children circle the picture that matches the word you say.**

Directions: **Have children connect the blossoms.**

What Do You Know?

1.

2.

3.

4.

5.

6.

Journal

Directions: Have children draw a made-up animal that has a **pair** of **wings**, a **beak**, and a **stinger**.

Story Words

flutter

tracks

stream

hoof

sink

prepare

ruined

record

direction

broad

Directions: Have children look at the pictures as you read the story aloud.
Then have them mark items in the pictures related to **flutter, tracks, stream, hoof,** and **sink.**

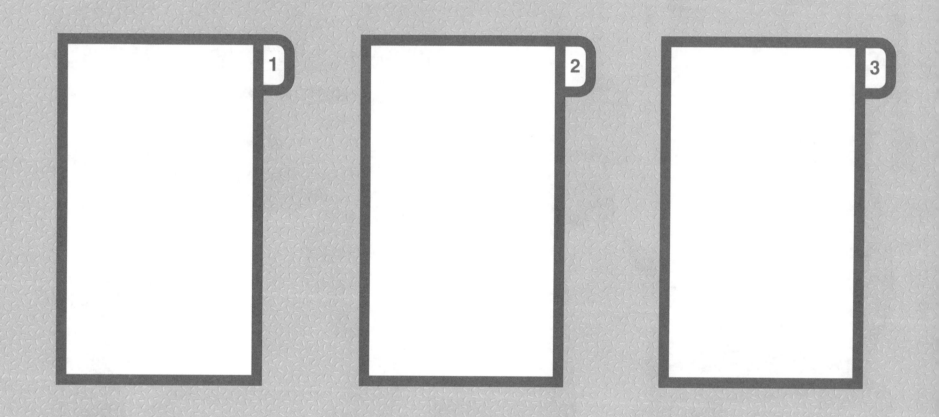

Directions: **Have children paste the pictures in the order they happened.**

Directions: Have children find and color pictures related to **prepare, ruined, record, direction,** and **broad.**

1. flutter

2. hoof

3. record

4. stream

Directions: Have children circle the picture that matches the word you say.

Directions: **Use an orange crayon to connect the things that are ruined and a purple crayon to connect the things that are sinking.**

85

What Do You Know?

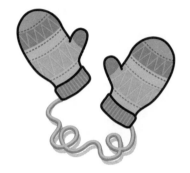

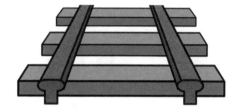

Directions: **Have children use the correct crayon to circle the picture that matches the word you say.**

Journal

Story Words

bird

measure

claws

dawn

release

demonstrate

capture

tangled

narrow

tube

Directions: **Have children look at the pictures as you read the story aloud.**
Then have them mark items in the pictures related to bird, measure, claws, dawn, and release.

2

3

89

Directions: Have children paste the pictures in the order they happened.

1. narrow

2. dawn

3. release

4. measure

Directions: **Have children circle the picture that matches the word you say.**

Directions: **Have children use a red crayon to connect the things that are tangled and a green crayon to connect the things that have claws.**

93

What Do You Know?

1.

2.

3.

4.

5.

6.

Directions: **Have children circle the picture that matches the word you say.**

Journal

Directions: Have children draw a picture of a bird. Help them label their pictures using at least two of the following words: **bird, beak, wing,** and **claws.**

Dear Girls and Boys,

Here are some pictures for you to cut out along the dotted lines. Use them when you retell the stories from the book. Don't forget—cut out only the pictures from the story you are working on now.

STOP

97

STOP

STOP

STOP

 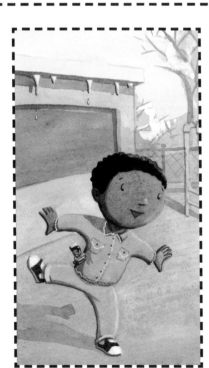 

STOP

STOP

Dear Boys and Girls,

Have a great summer!

Come back in the fall when Jordan,
Caroline, and Maggie move on to first grade.